A Penny For My Thoughts

By B. Anderson

A Penny For My Thoughts

Dedication

I'd first like to dedicate my debut book to God. He had a plan for me. A plan that wasn't mine. I wanted to write this book years ago but he knew I wasn't ready. I wasn't mentally, physically, or spiritually capable of putting together a book. God was there through all of my trials and tribulations, so all of the thanks goes to him.

Words can't describe how big of an impact you've had on my life Mrs. Wabbington. First, being my first grade teacher. Later, allowing me to job shadow you in 11th grade, and complete my yearlong internship my senior year. The kind words and encouragement, along with the text messages over the years have really kept me motivated. To be successful in this life and to make you proud. I also dedicate this book to you.
P.S. I will be reserving an autographed copy of my book per your request.

Last but not least, I dedicate this book to you Tia M. You inspired the title of this book because on a daily basis, you would actually give me a penny in exchange for my thoughts. When I sat back and thought about my debut book and what to call it, A Penny for My Thoughts was an easy choice, and it stuck with me. Thank you so much for the role you've played in my life. I will forever love and appreciate you.

Opening Prayer

God, I'm praying to give you thanks for making all of this possible.
Being there to help me through each and every obstacle.
I'm thankful for my good and bad times. If life was easy, I wouldn't have much to say.
I'm grateful for the platform to touch on some of those things today.
I compiled a small but comprehensive list of poems to give you an up close and personal look.
Poetry written over the last ten years produced this book.
I wanted to use some of my older poems to chronicle my life from a teen to an adult.
I pray I'm not judged for my thoughts.
I'm asking for forgiveness for all of my faults.
My goal is to help my readers learn from the mistakes I exposed.
To understand that mental illness is real. If it comes knocking, do everything you can to keep that door closed.
And if the door was already open, don't be consumed with its emotion.
Life's too short to label yourself broken.
Continue to fight. Eliminate the stereotype.
I pray that readers learn from the young black girl.
Open up their minds and show them that good fathers do exist in this world.
For those that have been dealt a bad hand, I pray my point of view provides a different stance.
We've all had our fair share of heartbreak. God, I ask that you allow their hearts to give love one more chance.
I pray that naive and gullible spirits are fought.
Men, love and affection can't be bought.
I pray that every barrier this book touches is overcame.
In Jesus name...

A Penny for My Thoughts

I wish we could take it back to when we first started.
Before any status or picture was liked or hearted.
Before feelings got involved.
When we texted all day and never wanted to end the call.
I remember when a simple disagreement was easily solved.
Giving all the free time our schedules allowed.
Being friends forever was what we vowed.
Had me gaining confidence ready to read my poetry aloud.
I remember when I enlightened you on abilities you didn't even
know you possessed.
Actually exceeding expectations, I can attest.
Reminiscing about the good ol' times.
Now I'm just stuck with my memories and the poetry. I keep reading
the same ol' lines.
Stuck, trying to figure out which left or right turn got me here.
No drink or smoke, but somehow I'm lost, intoxicated, and my mind
isn't clear.
Wondering if I hit a dead end when I realized feelings had been
caught.
Not sure, but there's a penny for my thoughts.

POV (Woman)

I always tell my side but imagine the poem coming from you.
I may understand better coming from your point of view.
This guy hit me up on messenger saying, "Damn you so fine."
I thanked him for the compliment even though it was the most common line.
He seemed real cool so I decided to give him my time.
We started off so strong.
Getting along, conversations on the phone lasted so long.
In the back of my mind, I'm still broken and stressed.
I thought my previous was the one. Honestly I still loved my ex.
I thought he understood me, so I looked at him as the best.
In return, all he did was cheat.
So as hard as it was, I knew I'd have to delete.
Back to this new man.
I was so hesitant, but he assured me that by my side, he would stand.
Only a few days passed, and he was already talking about being my biggest fan.
I slowly began to open up and embrace his plans.
Had an event but I was nervous to tell him he was invited.
But, when I told him, I was shocked because he got so excited.
His conversations ensued on what we were going to wear and us being the best pair.
He made me feel so comfortable. Forbidden secrets, he began to share.
That night came, I walked around the bar and spotted him sitting there.
We hugged and went over to sit with my friend.
There was something about him that separated him from most men.
Only thing on my mind was drinks and a wonderful night.
Everything about me, he seemed to like.
He made me feel safe, it all felt so right.
Such a fun time we had, then I took him home.
A surprising kiss he gave me really set the tone.
Days after, I started to feel sick and had a terrible feeling.
Never in a million years would I have guessed what it was, it would send us all reeling.
Nervous wondering what's wrong with me.
Going down the list checking all possibilities.

That day came and I went to the doctor.
My results sent me into shock because they were very improper.
Enough to effect anyone's posture.
My heart began to race.
In an instant, I felt like my new friendship struck out right before we took off to first base.
Feeling so terrible because I knew it would be hard to understand.
And the last thing I ever wanted to do was hurt him and ruin the plan.
I knew I had to tell him ASAP because he's such a good man.
I knew I was the one he respected.
So I had to be a woman and tell it and apologize for wasting the time he invested.
Please let me go, words he never expected.
That was what I requested hoping he could respect it.
Of course he was hurt and felt rejected.
Something I never wanted for us.
He showed me that good men are still out here, and he didn't come for lust.
I felt so bad because I hurt him, and he placed the blame on him calling himself dumb.
I tried to talk to him but I began to feel numb.
Now I see nothing but statuses and texts.
And all I want is to be left alone to get some rest.
Is he the one, or was he just a test?
Only God knows I guess.

My Story to Tell

Sometimes when I write, I write my life. I write about dreams and desires. I may key in on gold diggers, cheaters, liars. A strong woman or a deadbeat dad. Love, happiness, new flames, depression, or things that make me sad. Everything I write isn't my life, so don't take the bait. I write things that my readers experience because my main goal is to be able to relate.

I don't go to church, but I've never been to jail.
I'm probably not good enough for heaven, but I'm damn sure not bad enough for hell.
Trying to grow as a person and change the idea that I will probably fail.
I guess I just have a story to tell.
Trying to figure out why I have little to no friends.
When one does comes along, I do something stupid to bring that chapter to an abrupt end.
Repeated the cycle so many times that it has become a permanent trend.
I thought friendships last forever. Never break but maybe bend.
How much longer will I experience lonely nights?
At this point, I'd settle for constant fights.
At least I'd have a chance to fix things with that special someone and make things right.
They may look at me and question my vision of life.
I was diagnosed with Nystagmus so no one ever accused me of having perfect sight.

I see myself as a piece of bread they butter up when they need a favor.
They eat away and enjoy until I'm all gone. Then it's like they forget the taste they once savored.
Or, they leave me out until I begin to mold. I find a way to heal, just to fall victim to another's familiar behavior.
I feel like that thing they take a bite of after they pick it up off the floor.
Hard to distinguish pain now. I've gone numb from my body being so sore.

Being naive got me not only forgiving once or twice. Try three of four.

More chances could've been given. Who knows, I wasn't keeping score.

And then I finally get the point after nine or ten.

When I finally reach my breaking point, then comes the attempt at an amends.

Which prompts another month of disappearing in order to cleanse.

I'm Not Conceited

I'm not conceited.
I just set a goal to rid myself of low self-esteem, and every time I take a picture, it's a celebration of the goal I completed.
From far away, no one knows the journey you took.
They just look at the many pictures and proceed to judge the cover of the book.
They'd see all the stepping stones I had to climb if they took a closer look.
The self-esteem may be gone but I still take fifty pictures just to get the right look and the perfect pose.
No matter how far I go in life, I can still hear the names blind and cross eyed being thrown in my direction, it never gets old.
Just names immature kids used to make me fold.

I'm not conceited.
The dark days I overcame, some would never believe it.
At times, I still get nervous and won't look new people in the eye because of the way I was treated.
It could be perceived that me wearing shades is an added accessory to my outfit, or a way to look fly.
Nope, it's just a way for me to blend in with any other guy.
Anything for my eyes not to be mentioned.
Some people were born for the spotlight.
I never wanted to be the center of attention.

I'm not conceited.
Some still may think I am even after they read it.
Choosing not to accept someone's truth is nothing but pure hate.
Which is fine, I'm just trying to fake it till I make it to heavens gates.
We call names not understanding the toll it takes.
And we wonder why the suicidal totals are at such a high rate.
The slightest things can make one feel mentally defeated.
So please don't judge me, I'm not conceited.

Struggles of a Father

There are some things that arouse my anger.
I HATE when a child is forced to look at their father like a stranger.
A father is supposed to be the protector, a leader.
Not fill a woman's head with lies, get her pregnant, and play the role
of a coward and leave her.
I know we all make mistakes.
That's the area where we're never supposed to give up, we do
whatever it takes.
For most of us, it was a rough and rocky start.
But nothing can compare to that first picture they made for you in
art.
If you're absent, who will your son go to for advice when that first
girl breaks his heart?
Teach him to pick himself up when he falls, to never give up, and the
way to success is by achieving his goals.
You can't expect a mother to play both roles.
Be the one to tell your daughter about the games these young punks
play. To open her mind and keep her legs closed.
Boost her confidence by telling her she's intelligent, as well as a
beautiful rose.
Be there for every moment. Don't be a deadbeat.
You'll feel like dead meat once the truth comes out, and then you're
exposed.
Kids remember everything. They'll sit back and reflect and recall all
the lies you told.
And out the door goes the respect.
In their eyes, you should be a role model, super dad, the best.

As long as you're breathing, it's never too late to start being a good
man.
I can only say this because I experienced it firsthand.
Trust me, it's embarrassing when everyone knows more about your
son than you do.
I felt sick to my stomach when he was two. The only things I could
take credit for was a fresh cut and a brand new shoe.
I posted pictures the few times I had him just to make it look like I
was always there.

But in reality, I was stuck in a deep depression, my life was a nightmare.

I definitely loved my son and I cared.

No doubt about that. But I was scared.

A man in plain sight, but a boy at heart.

I had no idea how to tell mom and granny I was ready to step up and do my part.

They played the role of father while I was either entertaining women, depressed, or just didn't want to be bothered.

I never spoke up through, I just slowly began to play my role.

Took so long to get over the embarrassment I felt I was to my family, it definitely took its toll.

Five years later, I stand before you a dad who's still far from perfect.

But as far as being an absent father, I was not going to allow the jury to reach a guilty verdict.

I count my early mistakes as lessons learned, not a loss.

I'll continue to tell my true story as long as I have a pulse.

In hopes that someday, the stereotype that fathers don't take care of their kids, will be tossed.

Dreams, Nightmares, Dreams

Dreams
I kept having these dreams.
That I finally got consistent with my queen.
And we put together our team, consisting of four kids, maybe even five.
Buying us a nice truck, her being behind the wheel since I'm unable to drive.
Me finally being able to be the head of the family and provide.
Just us. No old flames from either of us on the side.

But then came those nightmares.
I gave up and developed the attitude that I no longer cared.
There was no beautiful house, car, or family to share.
In this depiction, it was no such thing as the perfect pair.
Tried to sway things in a different direction, but I couldn't, so unfair.
Countless nights, I tried to wake up and end it but I was stuck there.
I'm still stuck there...

Dreams
I spend all day trying to figure out what those nightmares mean.
Trying to get rid of them like deleted scenes.
I'd rather be planning on creating a bundle of joy that shares our genes.
I'd rather be going shopping for engagement rings.
How about planning a wedding for next spring.
But the plan can't proceed until these nightmares no longer overshadow that fairytale of a dream...

The Young Black Girl

The young black girl is the mother of the earth.
Though she is yet to learn her worth, she's the queen of the universe.
The young black girl has to deal with so much. She doesn't know what it's like to be a priority, to come first.
She lives in a house, but has never lived in a home.
All she knows is handling business on her own.
The young black girl got pregnant by a boy she thought loved her.
He told her all kind of lies just to get in between her legs. She would soon find out what his true colors were.
Her mom put her out as soon as the test was taken.
The young black girl promised to get her own place if her mom was patient.
She confided in her boyfriend just to have him split when she gave the news.
Sad and confused, turned into anger and loss of patience with being used.
The young black girl can't take another lie.
She stays strong even though she wants to break down and cry.
She sends text after text with no reply.
Homeless with no one to turn to, she goes to a shelter.
Praying to God for just one person to help her.
The young black girl has to face reality that she'll raise her child alone.
No job and no way to pay the bill on her phone.
She's been hit with every stick and stone.
And even still, she carries herself like a queen looking to claim her seat on the throne.
With nowhere else to turn, she goes to church to seek prayer.
The young black girl learns about Jesus Christ, her savior.
An apartment, a job, a peace of mind, are all the things she looks to set into motion.
Things slightly begin to swing in her favor, she sees the door beginning to open.
Still, she can't forget her depressing past and the fact that her heart is still broken.
Realizing the love she has for her unborn child, she continues to do whatever it takes.

The young black girl wants real love but will never again take the bait.

Making a promise to herself, two children without a husband won't be her fate.

Sex is irrelevant if a ring isn't in the equation, she's content to wait. Success is what she seeks.

Answered prayers landed her a good job, along with the opportunity to sign a lease.

She knows she'll be giving birth in several weeks.

The young black girl is becoming the grown black woman who did whatever it took to provide a life for her son.

The grown black woman is an independent one who beat the odds, and will raise her baby with the help of no one...

A Misunderstanding

I've been looking for someone to grow with until our hair turns gray.
I thought you'd be the one to stay.
But at this point, I'm not sure what to say.
We met one time, and I thought it was great.
You crossed all the t's and dotted every i, leading me to believe we could turn into soul mates.
Sitting and talking face to face, I thought we could totally relate.
Had me thinking about us starting a future. I looked forward to our own life to create.
I could see myself being your super hero with a black cape.
Out of nowhere, you developed an attitude and told me we needed to wait.
Your responses became few and far between. None at all or very late.
Over and over again, I rewound the tape.
If I did something, it would just be nice to know.
Yes, we're all busy but we make time for the relationships we wish to see grow.
I knew we planned to take it slow, but this is a stand still.
I'd just love to get your point of view, to see how you feel.
Was I someone to pass the time, or was this real?

The Response
From the beginning, a friendship was my only desire.
I wasn't looking for a spark, let alone a fire.
I'm not sure how many times I expressed my intentions. I finally grew tired.
The talk of us being soul mates caused my patience to expire.
You have to look in the mirror and wonder why none of your situations ever last.
You're overbearing with your requests, and you move too fast.
We met one time and I'm already the one you want to keep?
You give the impression that this is the way you are with everyone you meet.
You give off the vibe of a creep.
At this point, I think you're desperate. That's not how a grown man is supposed to act.
When you mentioned a child, I knew I'd never call you back.

Ten text messages explaining multiple ways to get back on track.
We hadn't even taken off, so there was nowhere to start.
There was no relationship between us so you could never accuse me of breaking your heart.
I did what you asked so please leave me alone.
I'm not trying to be mean, but don't let me see your number come across my phone.

So Much Pain.

So much pain spewing from a brain that can't be tamed.
When you're being taught your whole life to go against the grain,
how can you expect someone to take your last name?
Being told to take your bumps and bruises. Be a man, don't
complain.
When visible flaws are the cause of you being passed up for
deserved fortune and fame.
When a person is placed into your life to take, take, take, and you
have a strict mindset to gain.
That's a shame.
It's a shame that you have to experience so much pain.
When being a bearded black man with tattoos automatically gets you
sidelined from the game.
When a child's only example of a superhero is white. Stark, Kent,
Wayne.
Yes the laws may have changed, but the mindset remains.
Some still believe an entire race should be reserved for the back of
the bus or a train.
So much pain.
I stopped taking so many pictures because none of them fit perfectly
into a frame.
Society is consumed by social media, so likes and comments are
determining factors of being popular or lame.
Half naked pictures of a beautiful body is one way to make a name.
I can go on and on but the message is simple and plain.
So much pain... So much rain.
So much pain and you wonder why so many individuals end up
going insane.

Unlikely Ending

Someday, you'll search and finally find that buried treasure.
In the beginning, you promise not to go too deep, too early.
Remember those constant lectures.
But the love you feel makes you give in to the pressure.
You start showering her with dinners, flowers, teddy bears, and love letters.
As the passion grew, you began to go to extreme measures.
She starts saying things like, you deserve the world because you make her better.
By now, your heart and soul is all in and you think it'll last forever.
At some point in time, emotions started going up and down like someone was playing with the levers.
It wasn't as simple as it was when you first met her.
You find yourself asking for things that once came naturally like time and pleasure.
What once seemed so stable, changed on the daily like Cincinnati weather.
Feeling unsure of yourself because you didn't feel like you guys went together like salt and pepper.
Mixed signals on the norm made your brain think your heart had been severed.
Until that day she finally broke the news. Tears making your face wetter.
Letting her go was the last thing you ever dreamed of. But that angel needed to spread her wings, and you gave in and let her.

Life Lessons

It's crazy, the road we had to take.
All the good things, even the big mistakes.
It helped me separate the real from the fake.
I remember those long and lonely trips I had to make when I lived in the apartment with the lake.
Thinking about you, how we could've been great.
But I lost when I played around with fate.
Thought that just because I took you on some nice dates, every other area would just fall into place.
By the time I started to give you the love you put out, it was too late.
You were gone just like that even though I wanted you to wait.
I know it was the hardest thing to watch my heart break.
To see me be consumed with hate.
I always thought you were the cause.
But you actually did what was best for me when you put us on pause.
Of course those weren't the immediate thoughts in my brain.
As time passed, I realized that it allowed me to flush my foolish behaviors down the drain.
And for that, I forever thank you. You can proudly shoulder the blame.
It took some years but for you, I have a whole new respect.
So I just wanted to write this piece while I sit back and reflect.

Depression, Do Not Enter

Some of you are sitting around feeling like you're doomed.
Days filled with gloom.
Stuck in your one bedroom.
So much hate and disdain being consumed.
Reminiscing on great opportunities that were swept away with the broom.
Wondering if you'll allow new and current situations to bloom.
Your children observe closely and begin to be groomed.
Teaching them life lesson but can't march to that same beat or tune.
Feeling like you want to end it all soon.
But don't want your mother's eyes to be filled with sorrow as you lay in your tomb.
Torn, your soul is burning like the middle of June.
In two completely different places like the sun and the moon.
So many choices to be made, but not ready for the clock to read 12 noon.
Spectators looking on thinking your life is perfect, they love to assume.
Just wishing you could pause time and fix it all before hitting resume.
This was my life before I stopped the bleeding and closed the wound.

Chill Night

I write my feelings right in the thread.
No copy and paste. No need to duplicate the sacred words that I have said.
I want to be your good morning, and the last thing you read before bed.
When you got a headache, I'll be your pain meds.
Let me be the tissue that wipes up all the tears you shed.
I don't even have to write, just come unload all the thoughts in your head.
It's great to go out on a date, but on nights like this, we can kick it indoors and order a pizza instead.
Afterwards, I can give you a massage in a bath full of bubbles.
The perfect ending would be a great movie, let's just cuddle.
These are the moments I focus on making you feel special.
To show you that there is a such thing as levels.
And after the time spent with me, you'll never again have to settle.
I may not be the best but I can be YOUR best.
A real man comes to heal and restore, not to cause more stress.
So stop letting these guys fill your head with lies.
Just lay back and read these words before you close your eyes.

Chill Night 2

It's never been about having sex with you.
I just enjoy being next to you.
I'd settle for just sending a text to you.
Kissing you is one thing, how about I tend to the rest of you.
They always asking how I make this poetry seem so real.
All I do is talk about the way I really feel.
I write about us so it's not just something someone can steal.

Mentally and physically tired so all I want us to do is chill
Maybe take in a movie and enjoy a nice meal.
Staying on the phone talking about anything until it gets real late.
Just taking the small steps towards sealing our fate.
I wish time stood still whenever I'm with you because every moment together goes at a fast pace.
My chill nights were meant to be spent with you, face to face.
They always come to an end too fast though, leaving me yearning for another taste.
Only the ones that have that special someone can read this and relate.

Breaking Up Was For the Best

I've tried my best to keep my silence, but I've grown impatient.
So this is my closing statement.
Laying in my bed, it's pitch black but I'm seeing nothing but red.
Thinking back to old conversations and the things that were said.
Trying to understand old poetry I wrote while on those meds.
I have a lot going on in my head.
Wish I had picked anyone other than you. Maybe I wouldn't have so
many pictures to shred.
Anything would be better than writing another unanswered rhyme.
Afraid of calling the ones I trust the most and getting the voicemail
again because they're on the other line.
Yeah, when you're at your worst, it seems like that's everyone's
favorite line.
It pains me to make you the focus of yet another rhyme.
At first, paying your bills made me feel like one of a kind.
In the end, it felt like taking care of you became a crime.
Before you, I was stable with a peace of mind.
After you, I've been unstable in every aspect of life, causing me to
be in a bind.
True love, well true stupidity, made me ignore each and every sign.
Taking care of you had me full of pride.
But when it came time to return the favor and pay me back, access
was quickly denied.
It all came pouring out of me the day you left and I realized you
were never on my side.
I was your meal ticket. A luxury car that continuously offered you a
free ride.
My response to you prompted you to believe my feelings were dead
and gone, no they just had to run and hide.
You became a stranger to me that day. The hopes and dreams that
once existed died.
You lied, contradicting yourself just to get my heart and my wallet
open wide.
Your expired excuse was, you're broken, knowing I held all the
pieces.
You were so quick to pray to God for help, but ignored what the
Bible teaches.

You sold me countless dreams about happily ever after's, weddings on beaches, and hellos to a mortgage and so longs to leases.
I read that when I found a wife, I found a good thing.
So I could never look at you or your kids as a temporary fling.
You were my summer, winter, autumn, and spring.
I never imagined how much chaos and instability you'd bring.
But it's all over now that I've cut the strings.
I will be just fine. The question is, who will be the next victim on your list?
Six months removed from me, you won't even have a pot to piss.
From rent to your car note, from shoes to the watch on your wrist.
Stop me if I'm not speaking facts. The truth isn't considered a diss.

Thinking Out Loud

Looking at the things that consume my life.
Seems like people only care about a comment or a like.
I need peace. They just want to start drama and fight.
Where's my comfort? I see no one when I look left or right.
Tired of being alone lying awake at night.
Anxiety and depression reaching its greatest height.
It's a struggle to smile more.
I have family, but I don't know how to pick up the phone and dial more.
Time is ticking so I've been thinking about walking down that aisle more.
Looking for a way out.
Feeling like I need to go lay on someone's couch.
May be the only way I can add the confidence and subtract the doubt.
Don't read too much into this. I'm just releasing the tension my mental brought.
No canvas at the moment so I guess this is the next best way to release those thoughts.
I may be talking to myself though because I'm not sure whose attention this caught.

The Irony

It's funny how life turns out to be so beautifully scripted.
How some of us can smile, despite the pain we've inflicted.
A heart once consumed with innocence, turned wicked.
We spend years with no hope of the future, but in an instant,
someone can come along and get our spirits lifted.
How we can have the naive eating out of the palm of our hands, but
in the end, we're the ones that are left addicted.
How do we end up working dead end jobs when once upon a time,
we got straight A's and tested gifted.
Flashbacks presented a mixture of joy and terror as my mind drifted.

So far gone but we never remember the start.
In the past are once gloomy days that now shine bright, or a
promising future, now dark.
The only thing we remember is toasts to celebrations, or the
shattered pieces to a now broken heart.
Some days are perfect, others are tense.
When I think about it, there's only one thing that makes sense.
It was a blessing and a curse to be able to be on both sides of the
fence.

Schooling a Younger Me

It's disappointing that you haven't texted me back.
I know how you're feeling but I at least thought we could keep our
friendship intact.
I know your heart is all over the place.
But you make me feel like our whole time together was a waste.
For the second time, just disappearing without a trace.
My feelings were just stranded on third base.
I thought we would at least be friends forever.
Thought we finally had an agreement that at least those ties wouldn't
be severed.
You just gave me this spark.
I can't explain it but with you, I felt like I made the game winner,
scored a touchdown, and hit a home run out the park.
Without you, my days are dark.
I lost a piece of my heart.
You aren't just another one that bit the dust.
It was all love, no lust.
You're one a kind that was the plus.
Relationship or friendship, I just miss us.

Listen to me, I want you to stop playing the fool.
It's not your responsibility to fix these women's problems, you're
not a tool.
With each situation, they had you looking even dumber.
If she doesn't text back, delete her number.
You need to learn the definition of deuces.
Instead, you're out here creating excuses.
I sit back and can't help but laugh.
You're getting used, but you're also opening yourself up and giving
them the path.
You gave her two chances to disappear without a trace.
The red flags were all over the place before she got to first base.
Some people stay for a lifetime, some cease with the season.
If you need to ask why. Look no further than your current situation.
She's the reason.
Leaving her is definitely the winning play.
I'm not trying to jump all over you, I'm just giving you the blueprint
on how to score the right way.

If your days are dark, flip the switch.

Focus on getting rich instead of worrying whose lips you're going to kiss.

When the right one comes along, shoot to win, and I promise you won't miss.

Tired

Tired of being last.
Tired of coming home feeling like trash.
Tired of thinking about the past.
Tired of my son telling me I look sad.
Tired of thinking about what I should've, could've, would've had.
Just tired...
Tired of being sore from head to feet.
Tired of never getting any sleep.
Tired of family gatherings feeling like meet and greets.
Tired of never sitting down together just to talk and eat.
Lately, my girl's family been feeling the closest to me.
When this is read, that'll be the only line on repeat.
Tired of the realist things being recognized the least.
Tired...
Aren't you tired of being in a bind?
Being told that it's never the right time.
Maybe this isn't the best rhyme, but it's coming from a tired state of mind.
Guess I'll end this right here because I need to unwind.
These long days been having me in bed before nine.

New Beginnings

Just a little something from the top of my head.
I hope it's the sweetest, unique, and most loving thing you've ever read.
It's all true too, so I expect you to hang on to every word that is said.
My favorite thing about you is, you're perfect as if you only exist in a dream.
Every time I'm around you, I get the same feeling I got around girls when I was a teen.
Except with you, it's not temporary.
If I went down the list of all the boxes you check, this piece would be as long as the dictionary.
Crazy, how you stay on my mind, and we've only been on a few dates.
I know patience is a virtue, but when you're involved, I find myself having difficulty understanding that good things come to those who wait.
Don't get me wrong, I want to cherish every single moment, I don't want to rush.
But I do yearn for your kiss and touch.
It all started the first time I seen your face. That was the moment you became my crush.
Everything happened so fast.
My feelings and reality experienced a collision worse than a car crash.
I didn't realize that you were spoken for, my thoughts of us turned into shattered glass.
It may sound bad, but waiting for your union's demise became an important task.
And the day I found out it was over, my current situation became last week's trash.
The next goal was obtaining your number. I couldn't wait to ask.
Reassurance of my initial feelings became more apparent as the days passed.
Now, I can safely say, I'm not sure about the men of your past, but I can guarantee that you'll want me to be your last.
Poetry is my life so when it comes to rhymes, I have plenty.
I could write poems about you all day, so this will be the first of many.

Let me document our good and bad times.
This can be chapter one of our endless rhymes.
I promise to make you smile more and minimize the pain.
And maybe, just maybe, someday I'll be changing your last name.
Again, just a little something from the top of my head.
I hope it's the sweetest, unique, and most loving thing you've ever read.
It's all true too, so I expect you to hang on to every word that is said.

Ten

Today marks day ten.
It's so crazy because I feel like I'm already on my way to a decisive win.
I'm slowly starting to drain the thoughts of what happened way back then.
These last ten days have been wonderful becoming your friend.
I try to stay consistent and treat you with the upmost respect because I want our beginning to match our end.
I like you more and more with every text message that you send.
And your grade after ten days is definitely a perfect ten.

So glad I met someone who wants to take things slow.
We have all the time in the world to vibe and grow.
It's so easy, I love the way we just go with the flow.
Each day, I thank God because when you entered my life, I felt like he gift wrapped you in the form of a present with a beautiful bow.

So in closing, I would just like to say, the same energy I've given you thus far will be ten times greater once we've hit the one hundredth day.
I couldn't be any happier, this feeling in my heart is here to stay.
Let us be the best versions of ourselves. Just one of the many things I ask when I sit down and pray.

Disguise

I write to disguise the pain.
Hoping these rhymes can be a roadblock for the thoughts in my brain.
Endless tears have many t shirts forever stained.
I'd use these poems as my road to the fortune and fame if constant visits from Hurricane Depression wasn't attached to my name.
The year may change, but this sickness is still the same.
The people in my life decline and gain, but the loneliness in my soul remains.
I feel like the equivalent to a runaway train.
Despite my short fuse, depression has made me its favorite toy to use.
I've unintentionally become mental illness's muse.
Where is the sunshine? The 365 day forecast calls for endless rain.
I called out for better days. Only darkness came.
Depression has been a beast that hasn't been tamed.
These are real life problems that people have, it's not a game.
Husbands and wives become estranged, friendships have been strained.
I can only pray that one day, I'll never again have to write to disguise the pain.

Stereotypes

For most, it gets them fired up. For me, it makes me want to write.
Skin color, clothes and shoes, even weight and height.
Got people saying things so hurtful, it'll make you want to fight.
Stereotypes...
It could be as small as telling someone that just because they're tall,
they should play basketball. Or because they're short, they won't
succeed in the sport.
That just because I'm not rocking the latest Yeezy's or Jordan's, that
somehow renders me unimportant.
Judging women that had an abortion. And you haven't even read one
chapter.
Not realizing that rape could've been a factor.
Those of you who choose to ignore it, are just as bad as the ones that
choose to support it.
We've come so far from public bathrooms that our ancestors
couldn't enter.
But not too far because today, a white lady asked my homie if he
was a gang member.
Not sure if it was his shoes, tattoos, or his black owned hat.
Trying to frame it in the form of a joke didn't distract me from the
fact, deep down inside, she really feels that.
No different than how they see everyone that raps.
If he was to turn around and call her trailer park trash, you'd never
see anyone get fired so fast.
Just small comments like that proves they still look at us like we
should finish last.
Stereotypes...
They'll never see the light so how can we consider the future to be
bright?
A stereotype will mess up your point of view.
The smallest things will make you think you're better than me, or
that I'm better than you.
God forbid, I'm caught walking down the street at night with a hood.
I guess even when it's cold outside, I just have to be up to no good.
Stereotypes won't allow brothers to chill on the stoop without
putting them in the same category as those who rock nothing but red
and blue.

Police officers looking at those who droop. And when they go to pull up their pants, stereotypes got them thinking they're pulling out a gun ready to shoot.

If I spotted you with a close cropped haircut with heavy boots, would it be an accurate assessment to associate you with the skinhead group?

Or, because you're white, you can't jump, run fast, or hoop.

Tell me, how fair would that be to you?

Stereotypes are nothing but fake stories conjured up to make lies seem true.

Positive Vibes

Tonight, we're talking positive vibes.
Lately, I've been letting it all out because I have nothing to hide.
A couple weeks ago, I finally built up enough courage and touched on the subject of my eyes.
That was one of the things that once lowered my self-esteem and my pride.
But someone once taught me, with the right amount of love, you can rise above.
It's easy to walk above ground, but can you dig yourself out of the mud?
If you're reading this, I believe you can.
Whether you're a woman or a man, know that God has the ultimate form of a master plan.
You don't walk in vain on this land.
Right now, you may struggle with finding your purpose. Reading this is step one of that helping hand.
You'll be surprised what a positive vibe can do.
An encouraging word can have you feeling brand new.
I know we all love a new hairstyle and a new shoe, but aren't we sick of happiness that only lasts a day or two?
I know I'm tired.
I just know that coming out of the storm I've been through has lit a fire.
I don't want to just exist anymore, I want to inspire.
And if that means my words help you close on a new house, achieve a goal, or get hired, I'll feel like I've done my job before my body expires.

Broken and Shattered

I'm not worried about sticks and stones breaking my bones when my house is made of glass.
Shattering hopes and dreams, ambitions, and love affairs that started and ended just as fast.
A bone can be fixed, but can you ever fully repair millions of broken pieces?
My heart deserves an owner. It has a long record of broken leases.
Empty promises and broken agreements.
That can't be the definition of my heart's achievement.
I'm at my wits end and I'm ready to file a grievance.
Where is my fix?
A house on the market made of bricks.
A strong foundation that won't bail at the sign of something going wrong.
I've waited so long by the phone.
Starting to wonder if I paid the bill, as long as I've had to wait.
Praying each day that those sticks and stones didn't seal my fate.

At My Wits End

Every time I try to write this, I continue to erase.
Can't seem to find the proper words to say.
They told me to let it all out, but no canvas has that much space.
I've always been in a race just to find out that all the time I invested was a waste.
Can't blame anyone but me because the signs were always in my face.
I'm writing a new chapter and wondering if I'm finally in the right place.
I spent years starving for the basics and now, I'm finally getting a taste.
So I strive to be gorilla glue, not just temporary paste.

Came to a point in my life where I can no longer handle a lie.
I don't have the energy to constantly ask who, what, when, where, why.
I continue to wake up every morning sore, dry eyes, because I have no more tears to cry.
If you've never walked a mile in my size 10.5 Jordan's or Nike's, it's no sense in attempting to pry.
Pain and anger pick the worst times to consume a healing soul.
Contemplation enters the brain on whether or not I should continue to try.
Praying for my mind to stay at rest so I can finally enjoy my piece of the pie.

I can go on and on with an even deeper rhyme.
But frustration has taken up enough of my time.
The more energy I give to it, the more I feel like I'm committing a crime.
I see a healing coming my way in the form of a beautiful sign.
I believe it's God's way of telling me where I need to invest my energy and time.
Thanks to whoever took a moment to read the thoughts that are on my mind.

Where Have You Been?

It's crazy, I was looking for you like the US was looking for oil.
You're a queen so I only see you as being royal.
I'm loyal
But what makes my blood boil is the fact that we're in love but I still can't wrap you up like aluminum foil.
It sucks because I sum you up as a beautiful rose that grew out of bad soil.
A rough past but I want to get you spoiled.

I came into this situation just wanting to kick it with you.
Then I saw your situation and wanted to fix it with you.
I wanted you to know that no matter the flaw, you'd be accepted.
That you'd be honored and respected no matter how much my faith was tested.
That all the time invested wasn't in vain. Can't remember how many times I stressed it.
But heartache and pain can come to anyone that chooses to play the game.
I knew it wasn't the same as the relationships I jumped into with old flames.
Because even when you went against the grain, my feelings still remained.
Even when I felt like we were in jeopardy of not sharing the same last name, my drive to make you my wife never changed.

Embrace, Taste, Don't Waste

Embrace me
Taste me
Use me for good, don't waste me.
Help me remove the hundreds of invisible knives that are stuck in my back.
Accept the proverbial bruises on my face. So many times, it's been slapped.
Audition after audition for the greatest love story of them all, but no one could sign the pact.
Be my co-star and my one woman audience and substitute for all the ones that didn't clap.
Be my air to breath, fifteen years is way too long to feel trapped.
I've been lost for so long. Be my guidance, my compass, my map.
I've seen darkness for so long. Be the paint that brings colors to a world covered in black.
Embrace me
Taste me
Use me for good, don't waste me.
Twenty nine years down the drain, can you be the plunger.
Starving for love. Reading this, can you feel my hunger?
These temporary situations are going to drive me off a cliff.
Please take the wheel and be my Uber driver or Lyft.
I may ask for a lot, but I'll definitely return the favor.
Be my partner in life and I'll never be a traitor.
The flavor you will forever savor.
Embrace me
Taste me
Use me for good, don't waste me.

Where Do We Go From Here?

Consumed with anger.
Because I can't stomach the fact that I'm madly in love with a stranger.
Yes, I may know her first and last name.
But, I no longer recognize the beautiful woman next to me in that picture frame.
I'm just tired of our love life being considered a cat and mouse game.
Will our past ever be a distant memory? A platform to display the many obstacles we overcame.
Moving forward is a must.
Repairing broken hearts and regaining trust.
I miss the days when I would lift a finger to handle everything and it gave you a rush.
I'd love to get back to talking about our future plans.
But I know that a lot of pride will have to be swallowed before we can again stand together as woman and man.
So for now, I'm just stuck writing and wondering if we'll both take a loss, or will love ultimately win.

Change the Movie Script

You always feel like you're battle tested.
Until you hear something you never expected.
It comes out of left field and you never would've guessed it.
It always happens when you truly begin to trust.
When it's not just you and I, it's us.
When it goes way beyond lust.
And now, it's nothing but a look of disgust.
Trying to find that specific moment where you always go wrong.
Being told you're damn near perfect, but they all follow the same trend by leaving you alone.
You wanted to share everything and accept what's theirs as your own.
You did everything you could to set the tone.
And just like that, your kingdom is snatched away like a thief in the night, and you're knocked off the throne.
You look over, they're gone. Their name has been abolished from your phone.
Sitting in an empty place because this house no longer feels like home.
It's out of your hands.
Without warning, you have to cancel all of your future plans.
You lost your star player, so why are you still this person's biggest fan?
Because it went way beyond best friends.
When you looked at the score, the judges displayed nothing but tens.
Anxiety is kicking in. You see it coming but can't stop the same old trend.
Took you up to the highest mountain just to drop you like a bad habit.
They had you thinking the world was yours. In a split second, you realize you never had it.
A million thoughts got your mind crowded.
It hurts so bad but you try to be player about it.
Still wishing there was a slight chance that this was all a bad dream or a sick joke, but you seriously doubt it...

I continue to watch myself play the same role in a different horror movie.

Can't help but to ask, how stupid can I be?
As usual, I jump right in thinking God presented me the perfect gift.
I already know the movie by heart, I memorized the script.
I think I'm on top of things until I fall under the same old spell, then I drift.
I can't turn the TV off or change the channel.
The movie has consumed me and I can't find the control panel.
Am I the cause of my own failure? Or am I a part of a deeper scandal?
Before my eyes, I'm witnessing a new development in the plot.
Since I'm stuck in the same spot, I have nothing to lose. I might as well stir the pot.
I'm running out of time though. Can I solve the mystery before the next scene is shot?

Hurricane Depression

Who is Hurricane Depression?
An illness that continues to stalk me, as if destroying me is its only obsession.
I'm convinced, it comes back again and again to punish me or teach me a lesson.
I continuously ask myself, why was I the selection?
It catches me at my most vulnerable times, I have no protection.
If Hurricane Depression only lasted a day, I would be fine. Instead, it shows its ugly face for three or four, sometimes more.
It scratches at my windows and bangs on my door.
I pretend I'm not home, hiding on the floor.
My head is spinning and I'm spiraling out of control because I'm struggling to find the source.
Hoping that if I lay low for these few days, it'll run its course.
But instead, it knocks down my door and proceeds with force.
Destroying everything in its path with no remorse.
Finally, I've been found.
I can't move as if I've been tied up, gagged, and bound.
It won't stop until I'm mentally, physically, and spiritually on the ground.
I'm all out of fight so it was an easy knockout in the first round.
Broken, battered, and bruised, Hurricane Depression finally leaves.
I'm relieved but I know if I ever tried to explain it, no one would believe.
It's gone now, but I can count on it to reappear shortly after I heal.
With more joy and happiness to steal.
I'm sure Hurricane Depression has made an appearance at your doorstep, so you know exactly how I feel.

Anger Towards a Deadbeat

I keep asking the same questions with no answer.
You navigate through my curiosity like a dancer.
Why am I taking care of responsibilities you signed up for?
Picked up your slack the second I walked in the door.
Some men may consider a single woman with children baggage, I just wanted to be the bandage that mended an open sore.
Instead of taking away, I wanted to fill that cup to the tip, and even after, I'd continue to pour.
I'm not complaining, but why am I the one teaching lessons and providing knowledge to seeds that you planted?
You're upset with me because you treated my treasure like trash and took her for granted.
You thought leaving would bury her, but somehow, she still managed.
Again, your "trash" became my treasure and I thank God each day for the opportunity. I definitely took advantage.
I wouldn't put these rhymes in a category of disrespect, or recite them on a diss track.
I'm just sitting here reflecting on recent acts.
Please stop me if I'm not speaking facts.
I'm playing for keeps, you get no take backs.
I take pride in providing the shoes, the clothes, keeping "your" princess's hair and nails done.
It brings joy to my heart to go outside and throw the football with your son.
All the things you should've been doing but you just had to blow it by stepping out.
And still, "your kids" look at you as their hero. But instead of saving them, what do they get? A new excuse out of your mouth.
You're a bad father, a dirt bag, I have no doubt.
Remember, this isn't a diss.
There are just some events in life that shouldn't be missed.
The fact that anyone wants anything to do with you makes me sick.
I'm pissed and wish I had a remote that allowed me to hit rewind.
I'd go back in time and edit you out of this script and out of mind.
To reset, and I take your role and we all leave you behind.
So nobody would have to waste precious minutes of their life reading these lines.

Thank You Baby

When you appreciate someone, all thank you letters should go like this.

Dear ....
I just want to say thank you.
Thank you for giving me the time to vent.
Thank you for every heartfelt text that has been sent.
Thank you for turning broken into bent.
Thank you for showing me that you and I were meant.

No one is perfect, but you're damn near.
Your advice keeps my head on straight and allows my mind to remain clear.
I find myself actually listening. In my past, all I did was hear.
Phone calls with you are the best, but I can't lie, it'd be better to have you right here.
I may be in the driver's seat, but you've definitely been the one helping me steer.

I like the way we've been building this foundation brick by brick.
We're not in a rush, loving every second that ticks.
And to think, it all started with an inbox because I loved your pics.
A rough past we've both had. Thankfully, it looks like we'll be each other's fix.

When it comes to my favorite thing about you, it's hard to decide.
If I had to pick one area to describe, it would be the fact that you give off the most amazing vibe.
A long journey is ahead of us. Thank you for being the reason I wish to take this ride.

Sincerely,
.....

Broken

From the outside looking in, everything seems to be intact.
Only if you could see it from the inside out, then you'd notice the impact.
I'm a product of deep rooted issues that go way beyond the physical.
To a stranger, everything seems fine. Depression is invisible.
I try not to let my loved ones see the pain written all over my face.
So with everything inside me, I give myself some space to make it disappear just to continue to move at a steady pace.

Broken

How do I change the narrative when a life without mental illness sounds like fiction?
I thought about telling my story in the form of poetry and including audio depiction.
Would I be judged, or would they actually listen?
At least one person would be able to relate if I generated a vivid description.
This will be a Segway for the individual that believes they're broken and alone.
I was once that person and possessed the same tone.
Refusing to get help or at least talk about it, I used every excuse known.
Your entire life will begin to crumble.
It took missed opportunities, burned bridges, and lost friendships for me to be humbled.
Maybe this can reach you before it's too late.
When life starts to fall apart, don't take the bait.
Find the outlets that'll catapult you back into a positive mind state.
Use this as your token and one day, you'll be able to look in the mirror and tell yourself, you're no longer broken.

Final Farewell

I got up and wrote this because I couldn't sleep.
Some things I want to get off my chest, so have a seat.
I told myself we would never again be cool.
But time after time, you continued to make me break all my rules.
The battle between my heart and mind had been the ultimate duel.
For the last year, you've been the thorn in my side, but also my crown jewel.
Yesterday marked one year.
It wasn't even acknowledged because no one has been thinking clear.
Just wondering why my road continued to lead back here.
Sunday, it took everything in my power not to stare.
You had that undeniable power to take me back there.
All it would've took is one kiss and that's not fair.
When you sent that text, I accepted your invitation.
It's like all you had to do is be patient.
The more I tried to fight it, the more I got that sensation.
Just know, in a lot of areas, we'll forever be similar. We share mutual thoughts.
It's the reason I won't associate with you in any manner. I'll never allow new or old feelings to be caught.
Because of shenanigans, I can't see myself putting the relationship side of me back out.
It's way past the time for us to explore a different route.
Once upon a time, this poem had a different ending. I could never allow those forbidden words to grace this page or leave my mouth.
This is my resignation for anything you. This time, I have no doubts.
Most people would ask for a million dollars, a cure for cancer, or world peace, if they had one wish.
I would only ask that we never met, so feelings and recollection of you would never exist.
So with all that being said, I bid you one final farewell. I hope you get comfortable on my blocked list.

My Everything

My inspiration
My morning, my afternoon, my night.
I say it often, I'll say it again, thank you for being a part of my life.
Thank you for being the example, a role model, a gift.
Excellence, one of your many accolades, I wish I had enough pages to brag. What I have to say will never fit.
When I'm down in the dumps and feel like no one in the world can save me, you find a way to give me a lift.
You're the definition of a helping hand.
A one woman band.
You're one in a 900 grand, plus 100 more.
You complete me to my core.
I was an empty tank on November 3rd, and since then, you've taken that excellence and continued to pour.
I write in minutes what others write in days.
My inspiration, my everything. I try to express it in so many ways.
After 29 years of no you, I almost died of thirst.
So with that being said, why not consider you my first?
You are in a spiritual sense.
Marriage, another child, I was on the fence.
The possibility of another failed situation, I was definitely tense.
You being you killed all that suspense.
Thank you a thousand times for pulling me out of that trench.
You may get tired of my appreciation after a while.
But the whole world would be thanking you too if they joined me on this mile.

POV (Man)

I always tell my side but imagine the poem coming from you.
I may understand better coming from your point of view.
I noticed this girl because she gave me a few likes.
Took one look at her pictures, damn what a sight.
Based on looks alone, I knew she was my type.
So without hesitation, I proceeded to write.
Couldn't think of what to say, so I wrote, damn you so fine.
I was shocked at the fact that she responded. Maybe she liked the
fact that I was myself instead of coming up with creative lines.
I thought to myself, I must've sparked her interest. I didn't expect
one message back, let alone eight or nine.
We started off so strong.
Getting along, conversations on the phone lasted so long.
In the back of my mind, I'm broken and I knew she was too.
She had an ex that was trying to hold on, but I was determined to
give her something brand new.
To this point, my year had been a rollercoaster.
Just getting out of a bad situation so I needed a little closure.
Didn't want to focus on my ex though. Didn't want to hinder us
getting closer.
Deep down inside, I harbored feelings of being treated like a
sponsor.
When you love someone and that's how they make you feel, it turns
you into a monster.
But that got flushed down the drain.
Back to my new flame.
She was so hesitant, but I assured her that by her side, I would
remain.
Only a few days passed, I could tell the only thing she lacked was
the presence of a good man.
So I let her know about my plans of being her biggest fan.
She talked about her ex and the things he did. That fool had her heart
frozen.
But as time passed, I sensed the door slightly beginning to open.
On a random call at work, she told me about a Saturday night event
and eventually told me I was invited.
I couldn't believe it. I was embarrassed by the fact I was overly
excited.

I instantly started thinking about what we were going to wear.
I felt like we were a perfect pair and one picture of us would cause onlookers to stare.
She opened up to me so I wanted to do the same, it was only fair.
Telling secrets, it felt so easy to share.
We all have flaws but I saw perfection, I swear.
The night finally came.
Making a great first impression was the only thing on my brain.
I ordered a drink and as soon as I finished, she came.
One look at her, she was dressed nice, smelled good, very polite, the perfect ten.
We hugged and went over to sit with her friend.
Everything about her separated her from other women.
So delicate, honest, hardworking. I wasn't worried about the things she kept hidden.
She told me I made her feel safe, everything was going right.
Such a fun time we had, then she took me home at the end of the night.
A surprising kiss I gave her had me feeling like the future was bright.
Days after, we both were at the hospital for different reasons.
Mine had me slightly nervous. I thought she may have been sick due to the change of season.
Nervous wondering what's wrong with me.
Wishing they'd hurry up and call with results so my mind would be free.
I texted her but never got a text back.
Caught me off guard because that was a first time act.
She finally responded, with a message that had anger, sadness and confusion written all over my face.
My heart began to race.
In an instant, I felt like my new friendship struck out right before we took off to first base.
The only feeling I had was, wow, not again.
My heart was in denial but my brain kept telling me, bro, it's the end.
She told me I was the first to know, so I had to respect it.
Out of nowhere, she started apologizing for wasting the time I invested.
Please let me go, words I never expected.

I was distraught and felt rejected.
How could this happen to the one I selected.
I showed her that good men are still out here and I damn sure didn't come for sex.
I blamed myself. I found myself apologizing in each and every text.
She tried to talk to me but I think we both went numb.
She was the table and I felt like her crumbs.
Back to square one. Endless poetry and rhymes.
All I want is to be left alone to listen to sad songs and think about old times.
Thinking about my life, it's a complete mess.
Was she the one, or was she just a test
Only God knows I guess.

Letter to Arri

Dear Arrianna,

I promise to always be there for you.
As your daddy, it's my responsibility to protect and take care of you.
I want to create a family atmosphere that you can be proud to call your own.
You'll be my soft spot, the one that'll teach me to have a soft tone.
Your brother, my namesake has been my only thus far.
From the day he was born, I knew he'd grow up to be a star.
He's my star, you're my heart.
I want to make life perfect for you from the start.
Your brother grew with me and helped shape me into the daddy you'll one day meet.
He saw and had to endure mistakes I vow to never repeat.
One day, you two will be the seeds of me that are left.
I'm a work in progress but hopefully when you're old enough to read this, I'll be a vet.
I'm still getting the hang of things since I never had a consistent example.
My dad was a good dad, but since we didn't live together, I only got samples.
You've started to appear in my dreams
My curiosity continues to peak as I wonder if you'll receive the good perks of my genes.
I haven't met you yet, but I already love you to the moon and back.
You're going to melt my heart once you're able to talk and say it back.
I'm going to love you through your ups and downs, whether you're good or bad.
The first letter you'll ever receive is coming from the first man you'll ever love...

Me, your dad.

Closing Prayer

I'm praying for you.
That you succeed in everything you do.
I pray that you lead and only pick wise ones to follow.
Your next obstacle won't be a tough pill to swallow.
You're going to make it through like a champ.
I pray that happy tears are the only ones that leave your t shirt damp.
I can't see the future but I want nothing but success coming out of your camp.
Smiling is good for the soul.
I pray that anxiety and depression skips over you because I know it can take its toll.
I pray that you always stay young at heart even after you get old.
You are beautiful inside and out, I've been sold.
You, yes you. I want to see you experience how great life is.
Me believing you will win inspired me to write this.
In closing, I'm praying that all of your blessings are caught.
Thank you all for taking the time to read and embrace A Penny for My Thoughts.

Special Thanks

A special thanks goes out to my parents and step parents. They all had diverse but effective methods in raising me to be the person you see today. I thank God for using them to make me better. It takes a village to raise a child. They were and still are my village as an adult.

Miss Shatia Goodloe, there is no way I could have a special thanks and not include you. From the day you entered my life, you've been my support system. Listening to poem after poem, giving your input. Your constructive criticism, positive feedback, and constant reminders of my deadline, kept me on track. Thank you for being perfect. Thank you for being in my corner. Thank you for being you.

Quincey Montgomery, I appreciate you big bro. You gave me the blueprint on completing my book when I approached you about it a year ago. Thanks for answering every question I had, even if I asked more than once. I've definitely enjoyed reading your book on Kindle and look forward to many more. You have been a huge blessing to me. Thank you for allowing God to use you to help me.

God gets all the praise in the world. I got the idea to write a book at the age of twenty one. It never came to fruition because my focus, drive, and dedication was absent. God knew that I had to grow and experience life as a man before any of this could be made possible. I'm very thankful that he knows me better than I know myself. Thank you Lord.

Made in the USA
Monee, IL
27 December 2020

55672503R00035